HEROES OF AMERICAN HISTORY

IRMA RANGEL

Sara Cucini

LIGHTBOX
openlightbox.com

HEROES OF AMERICAN HISTORY

IRMA RANGEL

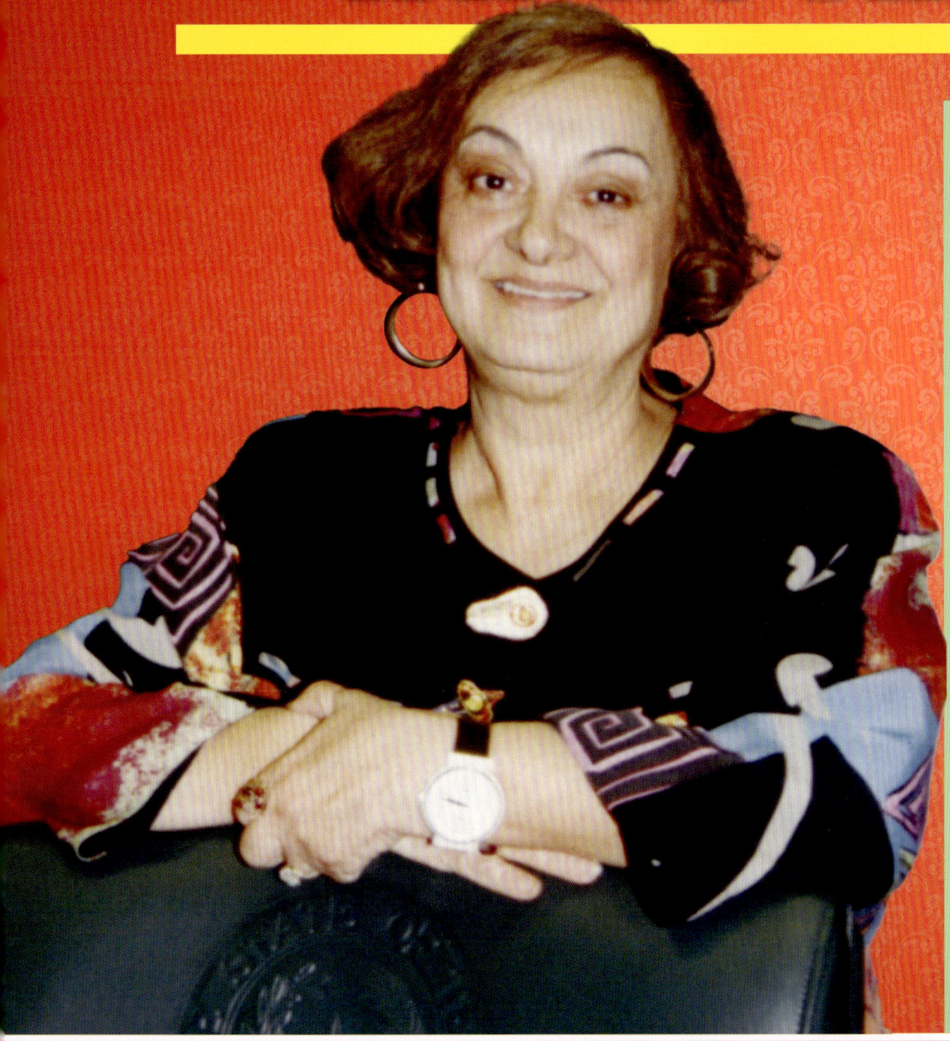

CONTENTS

Who Was Irma Rangel?

Irma Rangel was a lawyer and politician. She made it possible for many students in Texas to go to college.

Irma was the **first Mexican-American woman** in the **Texas House of Representatives**.

OLIVERS
JEWELRY
TaZoChel
KLEBERG COUNTY TITLE CO.
Oliver's DISTINCTIVE JEWELRY
Regional LOANS & TAX
KLEBERG COUNTY TITLE Co

Growing Up

Irma was born on May 15, 1931. Her parents were both store owners. Irma was the youngest of three daughters.

Irma was born in Kingsville, Texas.

Overcoming Obstacles

When Irma was young, few Mexican-American women went to college. Irma was different. She graduated from Texas A&M University in 1952.

1996
III
1996
II
1996
I

Helping Others

After college, Irma worked as a teacher. Then, she decided she wanted to help people in a different way. Irma went to law school. By 1969, she was a lawyer.

Irma was Kingsville's first female Mexican-American lawyer.

Working for Texas

Irma wanted to help shape how Texas was run. In 1976, she was elected to the Texas House of Representatives.

Values

Irma wanted all students in Texas to have the same opportunities. She wrote a law. It made sure that the state's top students could go to college.

Irma served in the Texas House of Representatives for more than 25 years.

Thoughts from Irma

Irma believed that education could change lives. She often spoke about its importance. This she learned from her parents.

"When [my parents] were discriminated against, they'd say 'Don't get angry, don't get bitter. Get an education and make things better.'"

– Irma Rangel

Achievements and Successes

In 1994, Irma was named to the Texas Women's Hall of Fame. A statue of her stands outside the College of Pharmacy at Texas A&M University.

The College of Pharmacy at Texas A&M University is named after Irma.

Irma Rangel Timeline

1931
Born

1952
Graduates from Texas A&M University

1969
Becomes a lawyer

1976
Elected to the Texas House of Representatives

1994

Inducted into the Texas Women's Hall of Fame

TEXAS WOMEN'S HALL of FAME

1997

Writes a law to help Texas's top students go to universities in the state

2003

Dies on March 18 from cancer

2024

Irma Rangel Young Women's Leadership Academy in Houston, Texas, ranked 23rd-best high school in the United States

Cause and Effect

Cause

Irma worked hard in school.

Effect

She became a teacher and then a lawyer.

Cause

Irma created laws for better education.

Effect

More students in Texas now have opportunities to learn.

SIGHT WORDS

Research has shown that as much as 65 percent of all written material published in English is made up of 300 words. These 300 words cannot be taught using pictures or learned by sounding them out. They must be recognized by sight. This book contains 64 common sight words to help young readers improve their reading fluency and comprehension. This book also teaches young readers several important content words, such as proper nouns. These words are paired with pictures to aid in learning and improve understanding.

Page	Sight Words First Appearance
4	a, American, and, first, for, go, house, in, it, made, many, of, she, the, to, was, who
7	both, her, on, three, up, were
8	different, few, from, went, when, young
11	after, as, by, help, others, people, school, then, way
12	how, run
15	all, could, have, more, same, state, than, that, years
17	about, an, change, don't, get, its, lives, make, my, often, say, things, this, thoughts
19	at

Page	Content Words First Appearance
4	House of Representatives, Irma Rangel, lawyer, politician, students, Texas, woman
7	daughters, Kingsville, May, parents, store owners
8	college, obstacles, Texas A&M University, women
11	teacher
15	law, opportunities, values
17	education, importance
19	achievements, College of Pharmacy, statue, successes, Texas Women's Hall of Fame

Published by Lightbox Learning Inc.
276 5th Avenue, Suite 704 #917
New York, NY 10001
Website: www.openlightbox.com

Library of Congress Control Number: 2025938119

ISBN 978-1-5105-8253-8 (hardcover)
ISBN 978-1-5105-8254-5 (static multi-user eBook)
ISBN 978-1-5105-8256-9 (interactive multi-user eBook)

Printed in Guangzhou, China
1 2 3 4 5 6 7 8 9 0 29 28 27 26 25

062025
110824

Project Coordinator: Heather Kissock
Designer: Terry Paulhus
Layout: Jean Faye Rodriguez